IGNORING
the
NOISE

FINDING FOCUS IN A FRANTIC WORLD

DOMINIC CURRY

Published by: Purpose Filled Publishing
a division of Purpose Filled Enterprise LLC

Library of Congress Control Number: 2017945937

ISBN: 978-0-692-89640-2

CONTENTS

DEDICATIONS

I would like to dedicate this book to a faithful few who have earned a place on the pages of my heart. First, to my wonderful wife... I have been blessed to have such an amazing woman stand by my side through many obstacles, high highs and low lows. She has been patient with my process and will be first partaker in the prosperity that my future brings. Words cannot adequately express how much I truly appreciate her perseverance and love. She is worth far more than anything money could buy, and I wish her well in all she does. I will always be the first to support each venture she pursues, with every fiber of my being. It is my true desire to see her succeed beyond what she could ever imagine. Life would not be as kind to me as it has been if she wasn't in it. I would like say to the world, I love me some Whitney S. Curry.

Next, I have to salute my two children who are the sum total of my wife and I's love. I am so blessed to be called the father of two of earth's finest young men. Christian and Joshua has the potential to be two of the world's most powerful men. I am not saying this only because they are my sons. We often receive complements many place we go on how well mannered they are. They are complete gentlemen. They open doors for women, they are well behaved in public and don't get in much trouble at home. At the tender age(s) of 11 and 7, they both already run businesses of their own and have plans to build their entrepreneurial reputation in and throughout life. They are both stellar students with the highest grades and honors within their grade level. In addition, they are full of fun and great ideas. I'm so excited about their future. They are AMAZING children. Please pray for them, that they may continue to grow into everything they are purposed to be. Christian and Joshua Curry, All I do is for you!

I have to take an opportunity to honor the world's most amazing mother. Jean Frazier-Johnson has proven to be more than worthy of honor. Ever since I could remember, this woman has made enormous sacrifices for me. Without her dedication, patience and attention, I would NOT be able to be a blessing to those I have been sent to bless. She is by far the best example of a mother. Not even once have I heard her utter a curse word and that in itself says a lot for parenting. She has raised other people's children as her own and has given my sister, Deonna, and I the BEST life possible. I owe her every blank spot in this book because she has certainly filled in the blanks for me my whole life. I love her beyond life itself. My "shero" ...MOM

Lastly, I would like to take this opportunity to pay homage to a special set of individuals that have graduated from labour to reward. I was privileged to have a few GREAT men that took time to pour into me without reservation. Though it pains me to embrace the unfortunate reality that they are no longer here to witness the fruit of their labor, it brings me great joy to consider myself a product of their selfless efforts and unfailing love. I guess I'll honor them in order of their deaths.

First, I would like to acknowledge my one and only Step-Father; the late Rodney T. Johnson. He came into my life when I was at the tender age of seven years young. He was the most amazing man I had ever known. He took on a responsibility that he didn't have to take on; to raise me as his own son. He was the epitome of a father. He taught me what it was to be man and more importantly, he was an example of a real man that I could model. He made his share of mistakes as I could recall, but what I learned most from him during the moments of his "mess ups" was not to ever make excuses. He owned his mistakes, acknowledged them,was man enough to apologize, and made every attempt to fix up what he had messed up. He was well loved and he loved everyone. He departed this world September 5th, 2000 and since the day he left, my life has not been the same but if he were here to witness all my success, I'm sure he would have been as proud as any father could possibly be. I am forever grateful for his leadership and sacrifice.

Secondly, I would like to pay homage to Pastor Horace Pitts. After the loss of my step father, Uncle Horace (who was actually my much older cousin) stepped up and stepped in. He played a major roll in a major way. We spent countless hours and number-less nights talking about the potential he saw in me. I would often tell him how much I admired and appre-ciated him. He was definitely a preacher's preacher. When I started in ministry, he would often accompany me when I would go out to speak and would cheer me on like a proud father. He took time to help me through many tough times in life and would always do whatever he could, whenever possible. To this day, I get so many complements on my choice of fragrance(s); I MUST humbly admit, Horace Pitts single handedly helped me to grow into a cologne fanatic. The world hasn't been the same since he left it.

Next, I would like to honor my Spiritual Father and chief advisor, the honorable Bishop Restine T. Jackson III. I honestly don't know where to begin.

Bishop Jackson was one of a kind. I believe God used him to help activate an intense hunger for reading and writing in me. He was an avid reader, great orator, and an awesome author in his own right. He filled so many voids in so many people's lives, that years after his death, people can't seem to let him truly "rest" in peace. His name comes up in almost every conversation. He made such an impression on those he encountered that he could never really die, because his legacy is ever present. He pastored me and show me how to be effective in the role. He taught me by way of example what the love of God looks like. I owe so much of who I am today to the enormous contribution he made in my life. I currently pastor the church that he established, and I initially thought to myself; I have some HUGE shoes to fill. Bishop made the transition process easier when he ensured that I wouldn't have to "fill" his shoes. He made it so that I could follow in his footsteps. Rest Well Bishop.

Finally, I absolutely, positively have to pay tribute to my dad; the incomparable Gregory W. Curry. Many people automatically assume that just because I speak so highly of my step father as well as these other great men,that my biological father wasn't in my life. That couldn't be further from the truth. I had an amazing relationship with my dad my entire life. I had the funniest and smartest father in the world. I inherited his wits. The man was so intelligent that its unbelievable.

He was an unpublished writer of so many wonderful books that I can't even count. He taught me how to fight and he taught me how to out think anything. He may not have always said things in a palatable fashion but he always gave the most profound advice. The love he had for his family was beyond measure and the life I could not imagine without him, has been my reality since Aug. 26th 2015. He would often express how proud he was of my sister and I and how we made life worth living. I truly miss our talks, his jokes, laughter and spunk. There will never be another like Greg Curry.

While many men dedicate many things to their forefathers, I dedicate a large portion of this book to my 4 fathers. Though not invincible, they are certainly irreplaceable.

ACKNOWLEDGMENTS

I would like to take this opportunity to thank some of the world's most amazing people for all their hard work, dedication and labor of love to this project.

To my awesome team :

There are no words that will truly express the sentiments of my gratitude toward this special group. This team really knows how to manifest a dream. I cannot and will not take full credit for all that has been accomplished. My team worked extremely hard and each of them are deserving of a special place in this book. I love and appreciate this group and if I had arms long enough, I would hug them all at once, to ensure they all knew that I appreciated them equally for their selfless efforts. Here's to you...

Antonio Martin
Gerrod Lucas
Deonna Johnson
Whitney Curry
Denise Lucas
Jean Frazier-Johnson

I must render special thanks to my scholarly advisors :

James Loving Jr.
Ida Jackson
Janel Frazier

Amazing Photographer :

Damion Brown
"Little Footz Photography"

Extraordinary Cover Model :

Zi'Ahir "Ziggy" Brown

Special thanks to the following for their help and support. They have supported this effort in ways that is hard for me to believe. I truly appreciate the gift they are to me :

Word Of Grace Worship Center
wordofgracewc.com

Lamar McIntyre

Tokeitha Wilson

Empowerment Station, LLC.

Seacret Direct, LLC.

Andrea Reider Design

Purpose Filled Publishing
"Purpose Filled Enterprises, LLC."

East Bay
Construction & Services1, LLC

PREFACE

The purpose of this unique, unorthodox, uncommon but yet convenient writing style is to unlock potential in the masses. We have heard it said, "if you want to hide certain things from some people, hide it in a book." At one point in life, I thought the saying was only applicable to certain sets of individuals... but as I have expanded my horizons, I have heard it said in many sects. I believe the saying has broadened over the years and has expanded exponentially. Primarily, because our world depicts an interesting theory; people would know more, understand more and would ultimately become more, if they would read more healthy content.

I believe the majority do not read because most of the information which is designed to help, often comes packaged in a form that hurts. It doesn't hurt physically, but it does hurt socially, emotionally and psychologically because life is very demanding for the majority. *There is not enough time in a day* one might say. Another might argue, we all have an equal measure of time in a day, and that is an excuse used by those who lack the will to do. My response would be, correct, we indeed share an equal measure of time in a day. However, the measure of time is not the determining factor in life. The deciding factors of life include to a greater degree, its series of circumstances which befalls us, that renders a significant contribution to the decision of what we devote our time and attention.

I have been privileged to travel to many parts of the earth, and I will say the story is the same all over. The world in which we live can be divided into three economical parts: ***The Successful, The Survivors and The Sufferers.*** Depending on the class in which you reside, will impact considerably whether or not you ***have time***. If you are among the successful, you probably own quite a bit of your day. You have what is commonly known as ***free time***... personally defined as *time without a demand*. For this group, it's a little easier to discover the secrets to successful life or the keys to improved living. The abundance of resources affords one the time to explore and embrace the art of immense success. I am not of the opinion that those who have, owes an apology to those who have not, neither do I believe they owe an apology to those who barely have. I just think that it is important to understand and respect each classes' perspective. However, I believe this book can add value to those whom are considered successful.

If you find yourself living in the category of the sufferers, you might not have any time, or at least it might feel that way. You are currently drowning in life's troubled waters, and the only thing that matters to you is rising from underneath the sense of suffering and making it to a place of survival. I truthfully don't expect many (if any) of the sufferers to read the pages that follow until they can rise from their circumstances. Although, if they could find time to read, I believe it would benefit them greatly as well.

There is yet another group that sits betwixt and between the sufferers and the successful and this group is known as the survivors. It is to this group that I dedicate the words found in the pages of discussion. It is to you that I devote my time and attention. It is this group that is often ignored. I call this group *the middle child of the world*, not as popular as the first born and not given an equal measure of attention, or perhaps isn't often considered like the helpless newborn. For this group, you're too rich to qualify for any assistance like the suffers and too poor to mirror the lifestyle of the wealthy and successful. You're not accepted or received of either party. You don't get embraced by sufferers because they think you have no idea what it's like to be in their shoes, and you can't attract the successful to mentor you into a new way of living because life has blessed them to the point that they have forgotten what it was like to be in your position. For you, life is a mystery because you only seem to fit in with the frustrated, miserable, and the confused. You are perplexed because you can clearly see that you're just one step away. You're scared because you're one pull from success but yet one push into suffering. You find yourself begging, begging for a pull up to another level of life and begging that those who have the ability to pull you forward don't decide to push you backward.

This position is a strange but yet commonplace for far too many. There are a series of circumstances which keeps the clock of life at a standstill. For this group, **there is no time.** No time to read, no time to study, no time to pursue, no time to sell, no time to buy. You don't know if you're coming or going, not sure if you're shrinking or growing. You are too broke to get tired and too tired to keep trying. You have many problems and few solutions. You know where to find the answers to your troublesome questions but the time investment is too expensive to spend it on the discovery process. Solutions have been forged by the gracious few that have shared them in ink. However, the issues and challenges of life remain because the answers for your life's equations are hidden in the vaults of many chapters, in which you don't have the *code of T-I-M-E* to access the secrets in these huge time-consuming books.

It is to you that I've been summoned to reach. Your class keeps our world afloat but yet, you are often ignored. You run businesses that the successful own, and your tax dollars pay the salaries of the public service members ,as well as, assure the welfare of the sufferers but yet, you are ignored. Someone has heard your cry, and I am committed to serving those who have served others for so long, receiving nothing in return. I want to give you a chance, finally, an opportunity for those who are just one step away. We might not be able to pull you completely into success with one encounter, but the idea is to give you enough each time to keep you from being pushed back into suffering. If you could be kept informed and engaged, one day you'll look up and see yourself as successful as you desire to be.

I am fully committed to writing a series of easy reads that anyone, anywhere, in any economic class can read at any of the *time* they do have. Readers can expect to gain a therapeutic understanding of successful philosophies that will help to shapen their destiny.

The Curry Experience:

Committed to the mission of helping others see a vision of a better version of self.

IGNORING THE NOISE

I think I would like to plant the first seed of thought based around a story from the Bible. I believe it would illustrate an attractive thought.

Matthew 14:25-30 (NIV)

25 Shortly before dawn, Jesus went out to them, walking on water.

26 When the disciples saw him walking on the lake, they were terrified. "It's a ghost," they said and cried out in fear.

27 But Jesus immediately said to them: "Take courage! It is I. Don't be afraid."

28 "Lord, if it's you," Peter replied, "tell me to come to you on the water."

29 "Come," he said. Then Peter got down out of the boat, walked on water and came toward Jesus.

30 But when he saw the wind, he was afraid and, beginning to sink, cried out, "Lord, save me!"

I don't necessarily want you to feel like you're caught in a sermon, but I do want to navigate considering a few things from the event found in the ancient script.

Peter will be our paradigm. A lot is going on in our story but what I would like to point out especially is, that Peter did a few things that most people aren't willing to do. Allow me to give you a bit of history that has taken place shortly before our story began…

First, Peter gets on a boat with some co-workers right after work, having been instructed to do so by one who is known to him as the best advisor on earth. I would imagine that things were going pretty well at first, and then suddenly he and his company of associates encounters a storm, midway into their voyage on the sea. They met a storm so great that the wind caused the waves to *beat up the boat*. The waves pushed up against the boat so aggressively that the boat at times seemed as if it were going to turn over.

I'm pretty sure many of us can relate to the story already. Maybe you were given some advice, or perhaps direction in and throughout life and at the start of things, much was ok, but at some point during the ride of life, things began to change, and from the looks of it, they were not changing for better, but rather for worse. I know for me, I don't usually question the advice of my mentors, primarily because I have the

uttermost confidence in their direction. I have witnessed their success. I have also been engaged in many
of their affairs, and for the most part, I have deemed
them worthy of my time and attention… I know that
it had to be tough for this group of followers to maintain assurance and pure confidence in a leader that
seemingly put them on the wrong course.

Could you imagine how they felt? They were only
trying to follow the advice of their chief advisor and
found themselves stranded in the middle of an ocean,
only to discover that the one who advised them to get
into the boat in the first place was away, up on a mountain top. Oftentimes, those who show and tell us the
way to success, seem so far from struggle. It's almost
identical to the story; One might say… ***"here I am in
the middle of a storm, fearing for my life, wondering
if myself, and my supporting cast will survive, and
the very one who sent us out here is away, far above
our frightening circumstance, up on the mountain
top."*** That is how I image the thought process of Peter,
and the rest of the faithful followers had to be at this
point.

Then comes the details of our reading (Matthew
14:25-30)

4 STAGES
OF GROWTH

V 25. Shortly before dawn, Jesus went out to them, walking on water.

I learned this principle in a leadership seminar offered by a company I partnered with many years ago. They taught me what was affectionately known as the 4 stages of growth.I believe it would be most beneficial to share. I'll give you the condensed version for your knowledge.

Stage 1: Unconscious Incompetence

This is a stage of growth that we all encounter. It is the stage of development when you do not know what you do not know.

After all, how can you possibly know something that you don't know? We all have things that we may very well need to know in order to reach our desired destination, but have no clue what those things are until we are informed. This phase is where you say to yourself, "I don't know what to do, neither do I know how to do what I don't know that I am supposed to do."

This is by far the most frustrating stage of development because everything in you is telling you that something needs to be done and to add insult to injury, everyone around you is telling you that something needs to be done, but no one has said what needs to be done yet alone how to do it.

Stage 2: Conscious Incompetence

This stage is where you find out the "what" and come to the realization that you do not know the "how."

This space in life is when you have to make a decision to put in some work. This is the moment when one's pursuit to personal improvement begins. You finally know what to do, and you also understand that you don't know how to do it. This stage is when you must make a commitment to your process of development. This is a moment of truth. Process is the place where desire meets action. It's no longer just a thought, no longer just an idea but it becomes a pursuit… a work in progress.

Stage 3: Conscious Competence

This stage of development is a very special one. It's a place of great reward. It's a stage when you know that you know! It's a point of confidence. It's where you will have doors begin to open for you as a sign of significant progress. It's the expression of experience. It's the place of certainty. This stage is when nobody on earth can tell you that you do not know what you know you know.

Stage 4: Unconscious Competence

Unconscious competence is what I call *the **Lamborghini of life***. It's when you do what you do so well that you don't even have to think about what you're doing, and you still do it exceptionally well. It's when you make hard things look easy. You make others believe that it isn't hard at all because you do it effortlessly. This is a place of great influence.

I digressed from the story to teach a lesson about the story. Now, Jesus came down from the mountain top, to check on his followers just as a great leader should. He gave them an assignment; He told them to get into the boat and go to the other side. Now, we have already discovered that His followers found it difficult to follow His instructions because it turns out that things aren't always as easy as they may sound. He told them where they would end up, but he did not tell them what they would encounter along the way. More often than not, leaders will tell you A&Z, they don't often tell you B-Y, because the details of life are the main ingredients of success. Great leaders can usually assure your destination as long as you don't detour the direction.

Jesus stepped off of the mountain right on to the sea. He was walking on the very thing that was seemingly killing everyone else. The leader is undoubtably in a stage 4 *unconscious competent* level of development. At this point, Peter and the crew are likely wondering if this storm will be the death of them, and here comes the one who gave them the orders to go out there, walking effortlessly on top of the storm that they are struggling in.

MEN FEAR WHAT THEY CANNOT FATHOM

V 26. When the disciples saw Him walking on the lake, they were terrified. "It's a ghost," they said and cried out in fear.

It has been suggested that F.E.A.R. could be defined as *False Evidence Appearing Real.*

I'm not saying that I totally agree with the originator of that philosophy, however I will say that it holds a lot of weight when it comes to the words found in the 26th verse of our story... when the followers *saw* the leader thriving in the thing they were struggling in, fear gripped their hearts. It is that kind of fear that produces false evidence. After they saw the success of the leader, while simultaneously seeing their failures; they *said* "***it's a ghost***". In other words, they made themselves believe that just because *they* were not succeeding that maybe success wasn't **humanly** possible. They submitted to their fears as opposed to their faith. Some people believe that fear is opposite of faith, and I must admit that I have in times past taught the same thing and truth is, I can't promise that I won't say it again. However, faith is what one believes and consequently, there are those who believe what they fear, even though it's false. I would say for the sake of discussion that, fear is **false belief** or **faith in falsehood**. You have faith in what is not, rather than in what is. I cannot number the times that I have seen this case and scenario. Someone gets a promotion that they have worked hard for and those that didn't get promoted (because they did not work as hard) will create reasons as to why someone else got it instead of them. The reason won't ever be because the other individual was better prepared or that they outperformed them; no, it's because they've done extra **non-work related** things to get the position. Maybe, someone has become wealthy doing the thing you do, and because you're not wealthy doing that same thing, they have got to be somehow, someway cheating the system.

Those are the kinds of things that were happening with the followers; rather than believing there was a way for them to do what they saw the leader doing, they decided to give into falsehood and call it what it was not; "*it's a ghost*" they said. They did not believe that this level of development was possible for all, and they confirmed their beliefs with their words. Men fear what they cannot fathom. They will create so much false evidence that it will appear real. Perception is one's reality.

BENEFITS OF
BORROWED BELIEF

V 27. But Jesus immediately said to them: " Take courage! It is I. Don't be afraid."

Before Jesus came down from the mountain, all the disciples were without a doubt right in the middle of Stage 1. They didn't know what they didn't know. After seeing Jesus do what was seemingly so far from their state, most of them never moved beyond the first stage of growth. Those that got stuck at stage 1, couldn't even conceive the thought of successful living. They saw what was possible but refused to accept it as a possibility for self. Therefore, the majority of them didn't even give themselves an opportunity to fail or better yet, succeed.

They never acknowledged the fact that the thing they ought to do was being presented to them. The 27th verse of the story suggests to us that the leader sensed that they weren't sure of the lesson, so he threw them a lifeline. He's such a remarkable leader, mentor and friend that he doesn't wait too long to extend some help with their test. The script says, *"**but immediately Jesus said to them; "Take courage! It is I...**"*

Wow! ... A real leader knows exactly when and how to guide. When a leader can sense that the followers are fearful of what they see, real leaders will start to speak. The reason is; leaders understand what it takes to succeed even when you cannot *see it*. When you find yourself in a place where you know you need to do something, but you do not know what to do or how to go about it. If you also find yourself in a position where you cannot believe it because you can't quite see it; please listen to those who are already doing it.

Jesus attempts to guide them through another sensual source. They would not believe what they saw, so maybe they'll believe what they hear, maybe they'll consider what he has to say. He gives precise tune instructions: he tells them to **Take Courage**. Courage means **to be brave**, or **to face difficulty without fear.**

Fear and courage cannot co-habit the same mind. When we find it difficult to believe what we see, it is imperative for us to borrow the belief of those who have exceeded our level of development until we arrive at a stage of complete awareness of our unbelievable reality. After he told them to take courage, he then told them not to fear. At some point, you have to decide if you're going to take courage or hang on to fear. As long as you believe a lie, there won't be enough room for your truth. Even if you do not yet believe; explore the benefits of borrowed belief.

DEMAND A
COMMAND

V 28 ."Lord, if it's you," Peter replied, "tell me to come to you on the water."

The teacher gave the same lesson to the whole class but somehow some way only one passed the test. Peter moves from Stage 1 gradually into Stage 2. I know it because, stage 2 is when you recognize the *what,* but you're not clear on the *how.* It's a place where you let go of pride, and you pursue progress. You seek advice, you seek instruction, and you seek direction. It's the point where you no longer trust your own opinion. You realize how far you have gotten yourself and to be honest, you don't like where you have led yourself. Something in you demands a command!

You get this thing where you realize that being grown does not mean doing what I want to do, living on my own terms, and listening to no one but myself. Rather, you understand that your childhood was a dress rehearsal for adulthood.It is a point in life where you need somebody to tell you what to do if you're going to make it.

Peter said *"Lord if it's you, tell me to come to you on the water."*

In other words; if this is the thing that I need to do in order to thrive in this thing that I am struggling in, just tell me what to do, and I will do it. Teach me how to do what you are doing so that I can live like you are living. I admit, I don't know, but I am willing to learn, and I am willing to listen.

This may only be Stage 2, but it is a powerful step in one's development. It's the embrace of courage and the relinquishment of fear. When you take a step toward seeking an instructor, you're sure to gain instructions because that is one of the first steps to freedom. Don't become satisfied with what you currently hear from yourself. Demand a command from another voice.

IGNORING THE NOISE
STEP 1

———

V 29 ."Come," he said. Then Peter got down out of the boat, walked on water and came toward Jesus.

The Voice of Choice

If we are going to graduate through the ranks, we are going to have to choose a voice of choice. Look how quickly Peter moved from Stage 2 (*conscious incompetence*) into Stage 3 of **Conscious Competence**. What is positively necessary for one to go to a place of knowing that you know, is ignoring all voices that will not guide you to your desired destination. For as long as you adhere to those voices, thoughts or suggestive reasoning, you will remain where you are and where everyone else is. The very place you don't want to be.

For Peter to receive the new instructions from his instructor, he had to be willing to shut off the fearful sounds of those who surrounded him. Once he was able to successfully disable the sound of the naysayers; he was empowered to enable the sound of success.

Isn't it unique how it doesn't take much to get you from where you are to where you want to be? There was only a one word difference between where he was, and where he knew he belonged.

Allow me to illustrate what I mentioned in the preface portion of the book. It will prove that you too are just one word, one thrust, one pull into the next level of life.

* ONE STEP AWAY *

V. 29 "Come, He said"…

Successful	
Survivors	
Sufferers	

I f you take a close look at the three lines above, which represents the three phases of economic life, you will notice that they are equal in vertical dimension, meaning the distance between each are the same. When I first saw something similar to this, I was blown away by how much (or how little) effort it takes to go from bad to good and from good to great.

Check it out; we'll start from the bottom up. Most people will do whatever it takes to move from drowning in a place of suffering to rise to a point of survival. That is a fact! Most people live paycheck to paycheck trying to make *ends* meet. News flash… they're ends; they're not supposed to meet. People will get a second job, work overtime, borrow, cheat and steal just to ensure they are out from a sense of suffering and are somehow surviving. They say it like this, *"I'm keeping my head above water."*

It amazes me that more people aren't willing to stretch themselves one more time, to the same lengths, in order to move from survival to success. Success is simple. In most cases, it doesn't require much more effort than it did to get you from underwater in that place of suffering, to that "head above water" place of survival. However, too few are willing to ignore the noise of their excuses, that they might acquiesce to a more progressive sound. Peter got that one extra push, gave it that one extra effort, and that effort was his willingness to change company.

It's one thing to tune out the negative talk which surrounds you but it's another thing to allow your freedom to call you away from toxic environments. An important step to competent living is taking a step outside of your comfort zone.

I remember so vividly doing a workshop for a group of rising entrepreneurs. It was a unique group; very diverse in every way. I instructed them to take out a sheet of paper and with a pen, jot down as many things as they could think of that would make their lives more comfortable and enjoyable. I was not in the least bit surprised when I saw some of their lists. I saw everything from family vacations, to alone time, business ownership, to limitless income and the list goes on... I went on to tell them to flip the page over and write down everything they currently do or possess that consumes their time. I told them to write down the things which currently prohibits them from doing the things that will make their lives more comfortable.

Go figure, I wasn't at all surprised at that list either. Everything that was *stopping* them from living a comfortable life were things they all had the power to change but lacked the will to change it because of a force called habit. I told the crowd, "*there you have it, your life is uncomfortable because of your comfort zone.*" I am still to this day amazed at the fact that many of the things that will cause our lives great discomfort is a direct result of our comfort zone. While the things that will give us great comfort, is one step outside of our mundane repetitions. We must be willing to get uncomfortable to gain comfort.

Peter chose to listen to the minority instead of the majority, and he did it. He actually did it! He moved from **conscious incompetence** to **conscious competence**. He was doing what his leader was doing. He walked on the thing he would ordinarily be sinking under. Those he separated from could see it, his leader was there to witness it, and more importantly, he now had an experience that no one could deny. He obeyed the right voice and got the right results.

IGNORING THE NOISE
STEP 2

V 30. But when he saw the wind, he was afraid and, beginning to sink, cried out, "Lord, save me!"

The Power of Focus

Focus was once defined as *direct attention or undivided attention.*

If we are going to ever move any further in our process, it will require the power of focus. Focus makes it difficult to fail. When we lose focus, it can cause us to fall into a worse position or condition than where we started. Focus is so powerful that when we lose it, we aren't remembered for the times we had it. Throughout history, there aren't many that even remember the fact that Peter walked on water. It is commonly mentioned that Jesus walked on water but not so much for Peter. Why do we think that is? More often than not, our failure will overshadow our feat. No one remembers the team that was winning in the 3rd quarter or the one that was up in the 8th inning. They remember the victors, the ones who remained focused until the end.

Focus is a powerful thing that can either make or break you and it doesn't take long to do either. Peter ignored the noise of those who surrounded him. He channeled his ear to a frequency that caused him to hear the voice of destiny, and he stepped away from fear and into faith.

He was successful in ignoring what he heard but yet unsuccessful in ignoring what he saw. Sometimes in life, what you see is louder than what you hear. He's walking on the seas and can't seem to control what he sees.

DISTRACTION IS THE SEED OF DESTRUCTION

If we are not careful our success will destroy us. So many with great success have committed suicide, lost their families, lost their fortune, and some even lost their minds... all because of the things they *saw* on the road of success. We at times lose sight of what got us there. Hence, we also lose the support of being there. Peter *saw* the wind and began to sink.

Distraction is the seed of destruction. A seed's purpose is to become a tree. Its great and bright future is trapped on the inside of its small, dark shell. If you are not mindful in little things, before you know it, they'll become bigger than you can handle. I believe it was

Babe Ruth who said: *"yesterday's home runs won't win today's games."*

We often get off of life's elevator far before we've reached the height of our potential. There is always more to learn. There is always another lesson that will benefit our future. The moment we think we have arrived, or done all that we were supposed to do, in comes the wind to remind us that we not only have the responsibility of ignoring negative sound but we are also summoned to focus by ignoring some things we see. It is a truth; action speaks a whole lot louder than words.

Peter got distracted and thus began his destruction. He found himself in a worst state than when he started. He failed to learn how to ignore the noise. All of the good he had done was sinking.

I was blessed to be able to go to what was then called *ground zero,* shortly after the U.S. tragedy of 9/11. I went to New York with a small group to do some ministry work around that time. I had the opportunity to visit the site and pay respects to those who lost their lives and to those who were severely injured. When we were there, there were news cameras, politicians, families, and officials of all sorts. I spoke with someone who appeared to be important and ask him…"what's next?" He said to me at that time, they were going to build the towers again. Immediately, my mind went back to when I was much younger, when we would visit that site. I could remember standing in front of the towers in awe at how high they were, and I could also remember at that moment thinking to myself ; construction had to have taken years to build. I then opened my eyes to see the building that I once looked up at was nothing more than rubbish and debris on the ground. It was then that I realized, what takes years to build doesn't even take a full day to destroy.

We must protect and keep our focus from any and all distractions so that we can prevent destruction. The good news is; while Peter was sinking he had enough sense and power to call on his leader for help. Jesus reached down, pulled him up and walked with him back to the place he had started. Distractions can take us further down than where we have begun, but God won't allow us to stay down if we're willing to get up, go back and start again.

The moral of the message can be discovered in the words of Jim Rohn, in his book *Living an Inspired Life,* he wrote; "*our lives are affected by two major things: one is price, and the other is promise. And it's not that easy to pay the price if you can't see the promise.*" Wow! What a message. There are many things to be said about this particular set of profound words fused together to create this amazing thought but what I would like to center in on is the very essence of focus found in these words. Germane to our discussion, we must understand that problems will always be present, but it is incumbent upon us to focus on the promise and not the problem.

The things in which we devote our attention consumes our time, therefore, it also secretly consumes our lives. If only we weren't distracted by our problems, we would have attained our promises. The good news to be told about our current set of circumstances is that we can undoubtably change the direction of our focus, anytime we choose. We can, at any moment that we are yet alive, decide to do something different, channel our emotions in another direction and devote some attention to what our heart says we can achieve.

An unknown philosopher once said, "*if you don't sacrifice for what you want, what you want will become the sacrifice.*" Many of us can testify to this truth. The things we had the greatest desire to attain has been sacrificed time and time again, all because we did not sacrifice for it. Instead, we've sacrificed it. Jim Rohn said *it isn't easy to pay the price if you can't see the promise...* either way you pay. Sometimes you pay what you did not budget for. You pay the high cost of your promises as opposed to the minimal price of your problems.

In our story, Peter's problems became more important to him than his promises. Can the same be said about you? What's most important to you is not determined by what you say, it is determined by what you do. It is what you focus on that will determine your destination. Pastor Andy Stanley said, "*it's your direction not your intentions that determines your destination*". There are many with good intentions that end up in bad places in life. Not because of their intention but because of their direction.

I can remember driving in my car. The city and surrounding area in which I grew up has this particular expressway that belts around three state lines in its sphere. I was in a rush. I would usually head south on this highway but this particular time, I was intending to go north for an appointment however instead of heading north, I did what I was accustomed to doing and went south. I was speeding, going in and out of traffic, bending the law, putting my driving record in jeopardy, trying to make it to where I was scheduled to be on time. At some point during my pursuit, I realized that I was doing a million miles per hour in the wrong direction.

My destination was not contingent upon my intentions. My destination would only be determined by my direction. And if I truly desired a new destination, I had to be able and willing to turn in a new direction. How about you? Do you want your life heading toward a new destination? If so, change your direction.

SELF EVALUATION

Many years ago I worked as a contractor for the federal government. Every so often the management team would come around and tell the staff that it was time to do what was called a self-evaluation. This process to me was mind blowing. It was unique because the management team had their evaluation of the staff, but it was not the only evaluation that had weight. They also wanted to see what individuals thought of themselves in the assessment process. Self-assessment is indeed a fascinating point of discovery. This process of evaluating oneself is genius in nature because when you examine yourself while knowing that others are also examining you, it should minimize the likelihood of delusional thinking.

This process ought to keep you honest or at a minimum, cause others who may be simultaneously examining you to take a closer look. It is important to know that you are not the only person watching your every move. However, you ought to be one of those who is evaluating you, during your process of progress.

One of the reasons I made the four stages of growth a big part of our discussion, is to raise self-awareness. We must know and understand that there are others who have already determined in their mind what stage of development we are in but it is equally (if not more) important that each of us look into the mirror of life and discover where we are ourselves and get laser focused on improving our reality. Life can be better. We do not have to live in suffering neither do we have to live barely surviving with our ***head above water***. We can live life walking on water. Seeing others do it is proof that you can do it. You must discover the secrets of their success and surge forward until you are living the life you've only witnessed with your eyes.

IF IT'S IN YOUR
VIEW, IT'S IN
YOUR REACH.

I'm reminded of two stories that made history: the first took place in July of 1969. Most of us have heard of this historic event, but many of us have missed the message that the story breeds. I won't tell it all but I'll share enough to hopefully help you get the meat of the message. It's one of the many stories of American history. The U.S. decided to allow a few astronauts to board a spacecraft affectionately known as Apollo 11 and it was said that these men would be the first to launch and walk on the moon. It was July 16, 1969, carrying Commander: Neil Armstrong, Command Module Pilot: Michael Collins and Lunar Module Pilot: Edwin *"Buzz"* Aldrin. They launched from Cape Kennedy in Cape Canaveral, Florida as hundreds of millions of people watched in amazement and with great anticipation. Some gazed to the heavens as the craft went into Earth's orbit, while others looked on with binoculars and other seeing aids. What they were witnessing was nothing short of amazing. The moon that they could only view with unique equipment was about to be under the foot of human beings. It took the crew approximately four days or so to reach their destination however, it was worth the wait and certainly worth the journey. I know it because Neil Armstrong uttered these words on July 20, 1969, after reaching his destination and accomplishing his mission… "***one small step for man, one giant leap for mankind.***" In other words; that which seems like a small thing for you to do can be the biggest thing for many others to follow.

The thing that they once upon a time could only see with their eyes was at that moment under their feet. What a testimony! What's in your view is also in your reach, therefore we must control that which we see because what we see will determine what we pursue. Even if others don't see it, we must be sure of what we do see and then pursue what we see. From this historic moment was birthed one of my all-time favorite quotes although it is unclear who the originator was,I pay tribute to the thinker that once said: "***don't ever*** *let anyone tell you the sky is the limit when there is a footprint on the moon."*

The next story that made history was unveiled May 6,1954, just over fifteen years before the previous story. It's the famous story of Roger Bannister. He was the first to go on record for breaking the barrier of the four-minute mile. The short story is; no one had ever gone on record for running the distance of a mile, under four minutes. At that time, the world record for a mile had been set by Gunder Hagg of Sweden approximately 9 years prior. He did the mile in 4 minutes and 1.3 seconds. Many had attempted to break the record in the space of 9 years and failed miserably. Many, in fact, most concluded that it was physically impossible to run a mile under 4 minutes.

It was a write-off, one of those things that the world just accepted as a physical limitation. Then comes Roger Bannister on the 6th day of May 1954, finishing what was said to be impossible in 3 minutes and 59.4 seconds. The crowd went wild before even hearing the official time. One journalist said as soon as they heard 3 minutes, a time under 4 minutes; they went crazy because there was hope beyond limiting belief… with .6 seconds to spare. He finished the race despite the noisy statistics. Needless to say, once he did it, countless people across the globe have achieved such a prize under the 4 minute mark. The current men's record holder to date is 3 minutes and 43.13 seconds.

The message found in our discussion which undertones each of our stories is simple. Just because it has not been done, does not mean that it cannot be done. If you can find it in you to silence even the quietest noise, you will be able to attain and then maintain focus that will catapult you into greatness. Close your ears to your peers. Stop allowing chances for your circumstances. Issue an assassination to your situation and win!!!!! You are so much better than what your life has produced. Tune out dream killers and vision stealers. Rise and take control of your goals and please understand your heart's command …. Ignore the noise!!!!

THE LOUD SOUND
OF SILENCE

This subject matter is near and dear to me. I have had the privilege of coaching many people over the years, helping them navigate through tremendous difficulty and trying times in life. I love the fact that often their answer was present the whole while, they just needed someone to ask the right questions. Through this experience, I have witnessed a recurring theme, people often tell themselves things that have little to no continuity.

Believe it or not, there is more said in silence than with words. I remember taking a class on communication, and I learned something that has yet to escape my mind. The speaker of the hour stood at the lectern and rendered some information that changed life for me as I knew it. He told the large attentive audience that 60% of all communication was non-verbal. He went on to say that 30% of all communication was tone, and lastly he uttered that a measly 10% of all communication was verbal.

Wow! Image that… over the last ten years or so, I have become fascinated with words, intrigued by the idea of language and the exceptional art of communication. This fixation on words caused me to study words and be a bit more cognizant of the words I choose to use when talking. You could imagine how I felt after hearing these gut-wrenching statistics. I mean, I have fallen in love with the minority, the group of which had the least amount of impact on communication…words. Only 10% of the things we say out of our mouths mattered in relation to communication. What the percentages suggest, is that to the receiver, there is more to be said about **what** we do and **how** we say things than the actual words we say. I think I would like to digress to ensure we are all singing from the same sheet of music. I want to explain communication from my vantage point. One of my mentors once told me that communication required unique skills, skills that will allow one to send a complete message without error successfully. Considering communication statistics once again. It has been said that 60% of all communication is non-verbal meaning that most of what you transfer to others is conveyed without speech.

Gestures, body motion, facial expressions, and such like, that are done in absolute silence will send more to a receiver than any other form of communication. Communication requires a sender and a receiver. It is important to note that many people receive what some do not even realize they have sent. Many people put far too much emphasis on what they say when we ought to be more considerate of the things we do. We have heard it said, "*actions speak louder than words!*"

Another thing to consider about the loud sound of silence is that sometimes, saying nothing at all creates the most noise. Have you ever had some unanswered questions? Have you ever gotten a portion of the details and the missing links created a louder sound in the midst of silence? I cannot begin to tell you the number of times I encounter people who have to be coached through the noise ignoring process. This concept has become quite popular for me in my experience.

I entered into ministry many years ago at the tender age of seventeen, at the brink of my eighteenth year, as a traveling evangelist. I would go far and near spreading the good news of the Kingdom of God. There came a time during my journey where things were beginning to slow down just a bit.

I wasn't getting as many calls as I once was and as a result, I was home more. Not necessarily *home* as in at my house but home meaning the town in which I lived. It was quite refreshing to be able to sit for a while and eat, rather than being the one feeding others. Then the new assignment came! During the times I would frequently travel, I had become the chairman of the youth and young adults department of my home church. It was an exciting experience starting to lead my peers, protégés as well as some predecessors in age. Boy, did I learn a lot about people and problems in a short while in leadership.

That was indeed the genesis of a brand new era for my life. The direction was shifting. I was being called into an advisory position; people were going to be depending on me for direction. This vein of responsibility wasn't necessarily foreign because even when I found myself in and out of places, whether it was as a general empowerment speaker or a preacher, people were counting on me for direction. The difference in my (then) new position was that these people would be present more often than not. There was no "*in and out*" it was just in. They were expecting direction, and they would be present for me to see their progress or lack thereof.

As you could imagine, this was entirely different from previous experiences. It was this position that would be the catalyst of change for me in the way I communicated instructions. In the beginning stages, I must admit that I made more than a few mistakes. I didn't always guide correctly and didn't always do what was right by way of example but I kept at it and was determined to improve my leadership ability. Fast forward time : I was elevated to the office of pastor in 2009, and this elevation brought about an onset of new responsibilities. In my former position(s) I was expected to do a lot of counseling but now it has gone to a whole new level. I decided to take classes on the subject, pursue a degree and study as much as I could about dealing with people and their issues. This course of study led me up a promising path. I was being called to speak as a mentor and coach just as much as (if not more) than I was being called as a pastor and preacher. The individual, one on one sessions morphed into more life guidance than spiritual instruction. I currently serve as senior pastor where pastoral counseling is the norm. I decided to share these small, snapshots of my more elaborate journey, only to make the connection that in the course of just about 20 years now, I have experienced coaching in the best of worlds. I have coached in business, life, and in spiritual arenas and have found that in each setting, there is a familiar theme. When people lack information, they manufacture the information they lack.

If they have unanswered questions, they often fill in the blanks with their thoughts and ideas. If they require pieces to spiritual or life's puzzles, they fill those voids with fabricated truths. One of the most dangerous places to tread in your mind is the place of silent noise. We tend to create the biggest pitfalls in life when we listen to the sound of created ideas. It doesn't often fail, I can just about bet that when people don't know a thing, they build upon ideas that lack foundation to soothe themselves of the agony of uncertainty. For us to gain what we long to attain in this life, we must shut out the loud sound of silence and await the appropriate response. It is in the place of silence where we at times, miss out on some of the greatest things life has to offer. How many times have you given up because an answer did not come quick enough? How many opportunities have we missed out on because we have told ourselves things we have not been told?

Many people talk themselves out of many wonderful things. We talk ourselves out significant relationships and great opportunities. Silence can be so loud at times. Maybe you find yourself often alone, and you tell yourself things like "*nobody loves me, no one wants to be around me*" or maybe you've been denied, and the thought comes to mind "*maybe I'm not good enough…*

Why should I even try"? There are so many sounds that silence will produce if we are not careful. It is imperative that we tune out the sound of silent noise and pursue those things that will bring us joy and fulfillment.

PARALYZING
THE PAST

The loudest silent voice in your present day is the voice of the past. Just because you were denied before, does not mean that you will be denied again. Just because a thing has happened before, does not suggest that history will repeat itself. There are far too many things that too many of us never attempt to do again because of an experience before. Oftentimes, fear of what has happened before, causes us to forfeit now. It is imperative that we become cognizant of the voice of the past. We must be sure that the voice of yesterday doesn't overshadow the voice of today. Many of us have been granted new aspirations which ought to emerge into inspiration that will lead us to our desired destination but more often than not, we yield to the voice of contrary thinking which was birthed in the days of yesteryear. When I am confronted with issues of the past, there are a few things I often suggest. This subject is a very touchy one because many counselors deal with people who have allowed their past to paralyze them, as oppose to the reverse. Without getting too deep with technicalities, paralysis can be easily described as **a loss of voluntary movement.** In other words; the ability to control movement has been detracted. You are unable to move what you want to move at the time you want to move it. More than we realize, we bury things alive. The danger in that is; everything that is alive will continue to grow. When we bury dead things, they disintegrate, but when we bury things that are alive, it grows bigger than ever. We can't use the *out of sight out of mind* approach when it comes to the pain of our past. We must ensure that some things are dead before we bury them or they will grow big enough to challenge you in a different form.

Let's take a few minutes to think about this with the seed philosophy in mind. A tree originates as a seed, but once the seed is buried, it transitions into its new form. Take note: it's the same seed in a new form. Some of us are facing some old things that have taken on a new form.

Some of us have been fighting the same battles over and over again, hindering us from actual progress. You would be surprised to know how far (or not so far) we've gotten all because we buried some things alive. We cannot allow old stuff to continue to hinder us from getting to new stuff. Even though we've been in many battles many times, it does not mean that we have gotten very far, particularly when we are constantly in battle with old things that shows up in new forms. The old stuff has us paralyzed, immobile, unable to move, stuck, living in the same set of hours perpetually. My advice is always the same in every case, paralyze your past before it paralyzes you. Cause it to stop moving before it causes you to stop moving. Embrace the possibilities of a better future because your past isn't half as strong as it seems. Your past didn't have enough power to live longer than yesterday. Its time of death was 11:59 pm, night before today.

THE POWER OF
FORGIVENESS

One sure way to paralyze the past is to exercise forgiveness. I am certainly no Greek scholar, but can recall many years ago doing a study on forgiveness and one of the languages we studied to discover a more therapeutic interpretation of the word was Greek. I don't remember a whole lot, but I do remember the word's transliteration was "***aphesis***" which transcribes as freedom or released from bondage. Forgiveness is often thought of being tied to one's emotions but to a greater degree, it's usually related to one's destiny. Contrary to popular belief, forgiveness is not about letting anyone or anything *off the hook*; it's really about freedom for yourself. It's about being released from the bondage of a noisy past. Some of us need to forgive others, while others of us need to forgive ourselves. Whether it's a person, place, thing or idea, we first have to free ourselves of the constant memory of unwanted emotions.

We need to forget it, and don't ever remember it again!

According to dictionary.com, one definition of forget is: **to fail to think of or to neglect willfully.**

Some things need to be forgotten to be forgiven. We can't always control what event happens in our lives but we can control what we do. Judging by the above definition, we have the capacity to neglect particular thoughts and feelings willfully. It also suggests that we have the ability to stop ourselves from thinking about some things. When we control what we think, and think about the things we want to fill our minds with, we put certain things that had us bound, in bondage. We in a sense, bind the things that had us bound and kill that which has been killing us. When we choose to forget rather than remember, our lives will drastically change for the better. The advice I gave at the top of this discussion was. Forget it, and don't remember it again. Let's consider what it means to re-member. In recent years, I have come to love words and ideas, phrases and compound phrases. One word, in particular, is the word, **remember**. If you take a closer look at the word, you will find at its root, the word **member** which in essence means to be a part of. Attached to the word is the prefix **re** which essentially means to do again. If we were a bit more conscious of our thoughts which births our actions, we would find that we have remembered more things than we want to be a part of us. We have taken the liberty of reassigning and re-attaching things that would be better off dismembered, dead and buried. We, because of a weak (strong) will, have not forgotten but have chosen to re-member things that are too heavy to carry into our future. No wonder we feel de-pressed or heavy laden. We have been given strength today, to carry the weight of our future, and some select things from our past, but there are some things that we have to let die so that we can live in peace without the loud sound of silent noise. No one can see it, and others can't hear it but yet it's been so loud in the ear of your heart, that it has stopped you from living a progressive life. Forgive and set yourself free by taking away the freedom of un-forgiveness. Forgiveness, in my humbled opinion is the most efficient way to paralyze your past.

ADJUST YOUR
FOCUS

When I was a child, I can recall the old folks saying things like, "*you don't get what you want, you get what you focus on.*" It is well understood that it isn't very easy to forget, but hopefully we are now able to see that we can choose what we will remember. Often, we make the mistake of remembering what's wrong rather than remembering what's right in situations. I want to challenge you to adjust your focus. One of the things I love most about being an entrepreneur is time freedom. I get to be a father who is present with my children and a supportive husband to my wife in all her endeavors. I recently went on a field trip with my son's class. He set me up if you ask me. He came home one day and said "dad, I want you to go on my field trip with me", and of course without hesitation I said, "sure I'll go with you son." A few weeks went by, and he says to me "oh yea dad don't forget the trip is tomorrow. We need to be at the school around 6 am." That was the first red flag. I thought to myself, 6 am huh…ok, we arrived at the school on time, early in the morning and then he drops the bomb on me and says "oh yea dad we'll be back around 8:00 tonight". As you could image, I was taken back by this new found information. I love him and all, but I did not expect to be out that long (smile). When we arrived on site of the trip, I quickly discovered that this was one of those day long nature tours. That's right, another surprise. I wasn't dressed appropriately, and as the day went on, it had gotten cold and guess who didn't have a cold weather kind of coat. I called my wife, and she came to the rescue. She brought me food and a warm coat. Anyway, the reason I shared this short story was because, on that trip, we had to break up into small groups. I had one group and one of the other parents that tagged along had another. Our group had to go bird watching for about forty-five minutes or so. We had to teach some of the children how to use binoculars properly. That was an adventure in itself. Some of these kids had no clue. The most common issue they faced was blurred vision. They were looking in the right places, but couldn't seem to get a clear view of what they aimed to see. As soon as I heard the problem, I already knew the solution. I said to them turn the wheel at the top slowly to the right until it becomes clear. I taught them how to adjust their focus, and I want to teach you how to do the same for your blurry situation.

Most matters have simple solutions. Most are not easy but certainly are simple. Life is filled with so many things that are seemingly important that it becomes difficult to get a grip on what should matter. One of the reasons why is because so much seems to be important, especially when we are viewing the world through other people's problems and other people's purpose. If we could live in a world that only showed us the things that will make the greatest difference in our lives, it would be perfect, but that is not our reality. We see other people's everything, and we adopt what's theirs rather than discovering what's ours. Therein lies the power of the focus wheel on the binoculars. What if I told you that the adjustment for you to see clearly was different than the adjustment for others to see clearly? Often, we are distracted by other people's destiny and more often than not, we miss the details of our own. We must figure out the appropriate method for ourselves to eliminate the likelihood of our sights being set on anything other than our own life's quest. That's another discussion that I'll leave for another time. I want to redirect your attention back to the power of your past and the importance of remembering the right things as opposed to those things that are unprofitable for our future.

Just like the view from the children's binoculars, everything is present, but everything does not have to be your focus. Some things are best left blurry. I know that it's there, but I can't see it clearly. We must ensure we gain and maintain control of what we focus on if we are ever going to live a progressive life. The power of forgiveness gives us the ability to remember things differently. Sure I've been sick but as a result, I have discovered the power of healing… sure I've been lied on, but as a result, I have also come to know that truth will always triumph in the end. One may experience pain and problems, chaos and confusion, misery and mayhem or whatever life may bring but through it all, in each area of weakness, you will discover the secrets of strength. It is in the undesirable moments that we reveal what we desire. We have a choice when it comes to how we remember; we can elect to select the memorable moments of our points of pain, or we can decide to remember the power we have gained in the process. If the art of remembering indeed re-attaches things, thoughts, and ideas, then I at least want us to attach that which made us the victor in it all, rather than the victim. We have the ability to adjust our focus to whatever we desire. Some would render the advice for us to try and rid certain experiences from our memory but I beckon for you to remember things differently.

We must intentionally tune out the sound that accompanies unproductive memories. If you truly get what you focus on, you must be intentional about your focus. If you concentrate on the victory, you will gain the victory in your mind, but if you focus on the problem, there will be problems manifested in your mind and emotions which will spill out into the days of your life. If you are still alive to tell your story, you have the victory and hence have the ability and the authority to focus on the details of your triumph as opposed to your trial. Adjust your focus and see what you truly desire to see.

Far too many of us major in minor things. We often allow the smallest obstacles to become our greatest challenges. I would never forget a full fledge fight I witnessed for a said reason as small as "*I don't like how they were looking at me*" ….. I thought to myself "oh, come on please people! Are you going to fight over something that you could have changed very easily?" Some of you reading this now have already judged and decided that they are the kinds of people who aren't good for our world but you made that decision without considering yourself. How often do you fight over *the way* something looks at (to) you? We fight in our emotions, fight in our minds, fight against our purpose and fight against the voice of reason which whispers the answers to our perplexed equations. We too fight because of the way things look even though it could be simply remedied. If you don't like what you are seeing, change where you're looking. After reading this, you don't ever have to fret because of what you see because you have been commissioned to adjust your focus until you see what you want and need to see for a prosperous future.

IGNORING *the* NOISE

FINDING FOCUS IN A FRANTIC WORLD

DOMINIC CURRY

Notes

NOTES

NOTES

_____

_____

_____

_____

_____

_____

_____

_____

_____

_____

_____

_____

_____

_____

_____

_____

_____

_____

_____

_____

_____

_____

_____

NOTES

NOTES

NOTES

NOTES

NOTES

NOTES

NOTES

NOTES

NOTES

NOTES

Notes

NOTES

NOTES

NOTES

NOTES

NOTES

Notes